The Pink Elephant In the Middle of The Getto

WORKBOOK

By TiTi Ladette

This workbook is not intended to replace professional mental health treatment, addiction treatment, or psychological treatment. It is designed to jump start the healing process by pointing out the inconsistencies in human thinking and behavior. If you suspect you have a mental disorder, a problem with substance abuse, or have been the victim or perpetrator of sexual assault, please see the resource information found in the back of the book.

Start Here

Counselors and addiction specialists have often used the term "pink elephant in the middle of the room" indicating there is something that is going on that everyone knows about, yet no one is willing to acknowledge. Do you know how big an elephant is? And it's pink?? Surely a pink elephant is clearly seen!

I chose this term as the title for my book indicating that the pink elephant is not only found in the middle of the room, it is also found in the middle of the ghetto. The "ghetto" is a figurative, Ebonics term for where you live. Your ghetto can be the hood, the barrio, the trailer park, or the suburbs. It simply means "where you live."

The Pink Elephant in the Middle of the Getto is not intended for one specific nationality or culture, just so happens that I'm an African American woman, so I could only write from an African American perspective.

When I initially wrote *The Pink Elephant in the Middle of the Getto*, my first thought was to tell my truth to the best of my ability, sparing no important detail. Writing the book became a form of therapeutic healing that allowed me to hold my head high and speak my truth to the top of my lungs.

Now that I have been allowed several platforms to tell my truth, I realized, after several attempts to send my book to various prisons in Texas, that I wasn't completely fulfilling my purpose which is to shed light on anyone who is living in darkness.

The term "living in darkness" can mean several things. It can mean living with any type of addiction or debilitating issue that has you enslaved, i.e.; drug, food, or sex addiction, mental illness, or various forms of obsession and compulsion. Living in darkness can also mean living with a secret of sexual, physical, emotional, or verbal abuse.

This workbook is designed to help you, whether you have been abused or have become the abuser. Whether you're addicted to drugs and alcohol, or whether you have a loved one who is. Whether you want to help someone who is living in darkness, or whether you want to help yourself.

Allow me to say that this book is not a cure all. It is just designed to get you "talking" and "looking" at those things that have enslaved you and have caused you to be less than the person God created you to be.

This book is your foundation to go on and seek that which will make you whole, whether it is a religious sect or church, therapy, an anonymous 12-Step program, or just renewed self-awareness. Whatever takes you to the level that you are able to function productively without resentment, fear, and baggage.

I invite you to grab your copy of *The Pink Elephant in the Middle of the Getto* as I will reference to specific passages in the book, grab your pen, and let's embark on the journey of healing together!

One of the things that you can certainly be sure of, this is a message that I not only share, but to the best of my ability, I live by, and so can you. Better yet, you can use your experiences to formulate your own message and find out for yourself whether your message should be shared with others, just lived by example, or both.

Let the journey begin.....

Unpacking The Past

The journey begins when you can actually admit the things that have been weighing you down, physically, spiritually, emotionally, and mentally.

Maybe you were molested as a child or raped. Maybe you have committed sexual offenses or have even felt a compulsion to do so. It could be that you suffer from a mental condition that you have not had the courage to get clinically diagnosed, yet you know it's there.

There are thousands of scenarios that I can state that could possibly fit any number of people. The fact is there is no one without character flaws. The probability of a person not having some issue or hang up is slim to none.

Truth is we can all work on something. I am a firm believer that there is a little bit of good and a little bit of bad in us all.

The first ideal is to look at those situations and write down those things that have been kept secret. The things you've told yourself you would never tell anyone. Then go on to view those things which may have been considered normal or traditional with which you grew accustomed to.

1. What was my childhood like?

2. What are some things that have happened to me that went against what I know to be right or wrong?

In the prologue of *The Pink Elephant in the Middle of the Getto* I began with a flashback of one of my early childhood memories of an uncle who came into the room I shared with my siblings and aunts to inappropriately touch my sibling. This was one of my first childhood memories. I remember feeling afraid and unsure, but I also remember getting up the very next morning to "tell."

One of the worst feelings in the world is to feel as if your voice isn't heard. After reporting this incident to my caregivers, there were no consequences for the uncle. In fact, he began to move my sibling from our bed to the bathroom where he could do his dirt in private. There may have been times when we, ourselves, have witnessed or been victim of unspeakable acts

3. **Have I ever witnessed anything as a child that I knew was wrong? Did I tell? Why or why not? If so, what happened when I told?**

4. What was I like as a child? Was I obedient? Rebellious? Shy? Promiscuous?

5. What are some things I did as a child that I knew were morally or criminally wrong, but chose to do them anyway?

6. Was I ever caught or punished for those things? What were my consequences?

7. **What form of discipline did I receive as a child? Do I agree/disagree with that particular discipline style?**

8. **How has the behavior I displayed as a child carried over into my adult years?**

9. **Have I suspected that I have a mental illness or chemical imbalance? If so, have I sought help from a mental health professional? Why or why not?**

10. **Who were my childhood caregivers? Was I raised in a two-parent or single- parent home? By relatives? In Foster care?**

11. How has my family structure affected my views of parenting?

12. What decisions/choices did I make as a young age that affected my adulthood positively or negatively?

Fixing My Feelings

In chapter 2 of *The Pink Elephant in the Middle of the Getto* I described how I was molested by a neighbor who injected me intravenously with cocaine. Although I didn't become addicted to drugs right away, I never forgot the euphoric feeling of the drug. Not only did the drug give me a feeling of euphoria, it made me forget every painful thing that had ever happened to me. It made my perspective of reality bearable.

Drug and alcohol professionals often refer to the use of drugs as a way to "fix our feelings." From my experience, drugs offered a temporary solution, similar to putting a Band-Aid on a bullet wound. When the high wore off, I found not only was the initial problem still there, but I actually added to the problem by spending all my money on drugs or with the feeling of self-loathing that came after the high ended.

Drug use is just one of the many ways we "fix" our feelings. There are other compulsive things we do to change the way we feel, like shopping/overspending, over eating, and others.

It is also important that we learn to properly identify our feelings. I have found that if I don't identify/acknowledge the true feeling, then I operate under the influence of a false feeling. This has often been the source of many problems for me.

For example, a situation could hurt my feelings. Instead of owning that my feelings are hurt, I will say that I'm angry. Once I conclude that I am angry, everything I do from that point on has to coincide and reflect anger. I could have avoided many physical altercations and arguments had I just admitted to hurt feelings.

A way to avoid false feelings is to change my perception. My feelings often follow my thinking. If I *think* a person is being rude, I'll immediately grab anger as my defensive feeling. However, if I say, "Maybe this person is having a bad day and is not aware that they are coming across as being rude," then I can actually respond in a way that is more empathetic and "let them make it."

13. **Have I ever used any drugs (prescription or street drugs including marijuana and alcohol) to change my feelings or my perspective of reality?**

14. **If so, what drugs have I used? How often have I used them?**

15. **Have I suspected that I am addicted or have become dependent on drugs/alcohol? If so, what are my suspicions?**

16. **Have I used any other compulsive behaviors to "fix" my feelings such as shopping, over eating, or gambling? If so, what were they?**

17. How has this compulsive behavior caused problems in my life?

18. Have I learned to identify my feelings?

Loving you/Losing me

One of the things I realized is how my childhood trauma and certain family issues sharply affected my ability to love and have healthy relationships. In fact, because of the damage, I continued to seek relationships that had familiar characteristics, such as physical/verbal abuse, infidelity, or emotional unavailability. As I continued to seek these relationships, I was actually adding more damage to the trauma I'd already experienced in my life.

There are some people who have actually come from great backgrounds and good family structure, yet find themselves in unhealthy relationships. Whatever the case may be, whether you are male, female, bi, gay, straight, or transgender, we ALL deserve healthy relationships. One of the most difficult things to realize is that until we learn to love ourselves, it is impossible to have a healthy relationship with others.

19. Have I ever settled in a relationship when I knew that I deserved better? Why?

20. Have I ever cheated on my mate or have caused my mate unnecessary emotional pain? Why?

21. What were the things that happened in my past or in my family structure that made me feel practicing or accepting unhealthy behavior in relationships was alright?

22. Have I ever stopped talking to friends or doing things that I usually enjoy doing because of my relationship?

23. Have I stopped practicing a religious or moral belief because my mate didn't practice it or necessarily believe in it?

24. Have I taken my mate back repeatedly after we broke up because of an infidelity or something we both knew was wrong? If so, why?

25. Do I believe I am truly in love with this person or am I in the relationship for convenience or just to not be alone?

Growing Pains

Sometimes we don't realize how inconsistent and dysfunctional our lives have been until we actually have children of our own. Often we pass down our belief systems to our children. Not just our religious beliefs, but our moral beliefs about what is right or wrong. We teach our children what to do or what not to do by what we do.

I passed down a lot of the same information I heard as a child. For example, a common statement told to me by my caregivers was, "Don't do as I do, do as I say!" Unfortunately, our children will more than likely do what we do. In this section, I wanted to explore how we ourselves were shaped by the caregivers who raised us and how we in turn shape our children.

We will explore the values and beliefs passed on to our children. Once we get a good look at these values and beliefs- we have an opportunity to decide which of them are worth keeping because we believe in them, or which ones we don't really believe, but pass down because they were passed down from our childhood caregivers.

26. What are some beliefs that have been traditionally passed down in my family, for example religious, moral, or social beliefs?

27. Do I teach my children these beliefs and values?

28. How do I respond when people around me do not subscribe to my beliefs?

29. What beliefs have I practiced simply because I was "taught to" but don't necessarily believe in?

30. Have I accepted the fact that my children will eventually grow up and find their own beliefs and values? Have I accepted the fact that everyone has the right to choose their own beliefs?

Growing Up In Public

"Growing up in public" is a term often used to describe the process in which you mature in a way that is visibly obvious to others. As adorable as it may sound, it's not always a pretty process. Often people will not only see our growth in its aftermath, they will see our struggles, our mistakes, and our failures along our path to growth.

The great thing about growing up in public is that it adds positive substance to the continuum of our universe. It gives others identification with their own process and hope that if the outcome was growth for you, then it can be for them as well.

Most healthy organisms that grow require food and sunlight. In this section we will get a chance to look at some of the mistakes us as humans have made, the valuable lessons we've learned, and a chance to see that everything happens for a reason whether or not the reason is immediately revealed to us.

This section will hopefully provide us sunlight by writing down our mistakes so that they are no longer holding us hostage and the emotional "food" we need to grow.

One of the ways we can acknowledge our growth is when we can forgive ourselves for past mistakes.

A friend of mine used to always say, "We need to learn to move from shame to guilt-shame means I AM a mistake, guilt means I MADE a mistake, and when we are guilty, then we can forgive ourselves."

As much as we feel the world, society, and the people around us judge us, we need to realize that we are often our own worst critics. We should learn to not be so hard on ourselves. We must realize that *everyone* makes mistakes. Although the mistakes differ in degrees of seriousness and consequences, the hope is that we *can* learn from them. One of the things I strive to do is to NOT make the same mistake twice.

31. What mistakes have I made that cause me to feel the most shame, remorse, or guilt?

32. Have I made amends for the mistake or attempted to make it right?

33. What can I do to ensure I don't make the same mistake again?

34. Have I ever lied about something that caused someone else to be punished for something they didn't do?

35. Do I believe that I can be forgiven for my mistakes? Do I believe that I can forgive myself for my mistakes? Why or why not?

A Prayer and a Plan

I have often been questioned regarding my religious beliefs. My answer remains the same. I don't subscribe to religion. Instead, I subscribe to spirituality. I follow Christian principles and believe, no, I KNOW there is a God, a supreme, mighty creator who rescued me from myself.

Whether you claim a religion or choose not to believe, everyone in this world believes in something. Even if it's scientology or atheism, that is still a belief. I've read in another literary masterpiece that any form of communication with a higher power or supreme being is *prayer.*

At times, I've even thought that I was mad at God and refused to pray. I didn't realize that by thinking this to myself, I was in a sense praying.

Contrary to popular belief, prayer doesn't have to be formal. It doesn't have to be done on your knees, in a closet, or by using eloquent words of religious doctrine. We can pray out loud or to ourselves. We can get down on our knees or not. We can pray in the shower, while driving, etc. The most important thing to me is that we pray. We ask for strength, help, and guidance. We pray for others and we pray for the world we live in.

Nothing beats prayer. I am a firm believer that prayer changes things. I grew up with my Grandmother's God, the God I was taught about as a child. When I made it to the rooms of Narcotics Anonymous, I was offered the chance to re define my understanding of God. I needed to know that God would not strike me down for my mistakes, but instead love me and re-direct me.

As I began to form a personal relationship with God, I began to realize how important prayer is to my well-being.

There are times when I get in self-will and don't consult the God of my understanding about my life and the decisions in my life. Those are the times I seem to make the most mistakes.

I have learned to pray about everything. I pray about my business and personal decisions. I pray about what to say, what to wear, and what to do. I pray for others and I pray for myself.

People have often referred to me as the "come up Queen." No one ever really understood how I could go from being on the streets and in a matter of months have a job, a car, and a house. This was a repeated cycle.

This has always been an easy thing to do. I have often said, "I can *get* anything, I just can't *keep* it!"

This time around there was something different. I didn't want to get the job, the car, and the house. I wanted to do something to make amends to the universe for being so selfish and taking life for granted. I wanted to make amends to the people who love me most whom I seemed to have hurt the most. I wanted to give back and create such a change that those others who have faced my dilemma with drug addiction and mental illness didn't have to make the same mistakes I did. I also wanted to be an inspiration to *everyone* so that anyone who was not living their dream or up to their full potential could understand that it doesn't matter where you've come from or what you've been through, you can be successful and live up to your potential.

In chapter four of *The Pink Elephant in the Middle of the Getto*, I mentioned one of the most monumental moments of my life; the time I'd actually stabbed someone in a fit of rage.

This was life changing for me. I ended up doing a two year sentence in prison. Before going, I pleaded with God not to allow me to be sentenced to prison but instead allow me to get probation or be found "not guilty."

My prayer to God during the first few months I awaited trial was filled with a rational, intellectual prayer. I was stating facts and justifying to God why he should allow me to evade the punishment the judicial system was seeking for my crime. Seven months later it became apparent that I was not going to get off without a punishment. By God's grace, the fifteen year aggravated sentence the judge initially presented was reduced to a two year aggravated sentence.

When I was told it was my last chance to either sign for the two year sentence or face a trial before a jury, I decided to think about it over the weekend, and then give my lawyer my final decision the following Monday.

At this time, my prayer went from an intellectual conversation to a plea. I was pleading with God to send a miracle so that I could avoid having to go to prison. I tell people all the time that God spoke to me. I didn't hear his reply with my ears. I heard it with my heart.

I questioned God, "God, why do I have to do time in prison?" and God spoke to my heart and said, "Because you did it."

In that moment, I was able to go back over my life and take responsibility for the decisions I made from the time in my life I knew right from wrong. I vowed that when I got to prison I wasn't going to participate in foolishness. I was going to read, write, and pray.

That is where I came up with a prayer and a plan. I prayed for forgiveness, for strength, and for guidance. I actually prayed for a plan to help me succeed and make a difference when I returned to the outside world.

The one thing I know. There is nothing that is more powerful than a person with a prayer and a plan.

Let's conclude this portion of our journey by gathering all the things we've realized about ourselves in this workbook, praying to the God of our understanding about these things, then moving forward by creating a personal plan for our lives.

36. What is something that was revealed to me during the course of this workbook?

37. Have I found anything in which I need to forgive myself for? If so, what is it?

38. Have I found anything that I need to forgive others for? If so, what is it?

39. Do I believe that prayer can help me change my thoughts, actions, and behavior? Why or why not?

40. Have I established a relationship with the God of my understanding? Why or why not?

41. What exactly do I believe about God or a supreme, higher power?

42. Whatever my belief, does this power have the ability to help me in times of trouble, distress, or sickness?

43. In what ways can the God of my understanding or this supreme, higher power help me to become productive or successful?

44. Is there something I have always wanted to do, but have never had the courage or resources to do it? If so, what?

45. How can prayer and a belief in God or supreme, higher power help me to accomplish this?

46. Have I taken the time to write down my goals by categorizing them as short term, mid-range, and long term goals?

On this page feel free to write down your goals for your future. Include the things you want to accomplish now, later, and in the future.

Goals

Short-Term	Mid-Range	Long-Term

47. Have I devised a plan of action to achieve each of these goals? (If not, please take a moment to create a plan of action to achieve short term, mid-range, and long term goals. For example, if your goal is to go back to school, what documents do you need to obtain? Have you visited the school campus and talked with an administrator? Have you filed for financial aid or applied for scholarships?)

On the following page, write down your plan of action to complete your goals. I find it helpful to do at least one thing daily from my plan of action to reach my goal.

Plan of action to obtain:

Short –Term Goals:

Mid-Range Goals:

Long-Term Goals:

48. Am I willing to incorporate prayer and a relationship with God or a supreme, higher power in my life? Why or why not?

49. Have I realized by working this workbook that I need additional help or support with any issues such as addiction, overeating, gambling, sex, etc.?

50. Am I willing to seek help for the issues that have been revealed? (If so, please go back and list this as a goal!)

Final Note to My Readers

I want to take the time to thank you for completing this work book. I hope that you have been helped in some way. I assure you the questions in this book are the questions I have answered myself at one point, and by doing so, have been able to take the realizations that derived from my answers, and have been able to move forward in my life.

I have learned so much during the past few years, not only in my college courses that deal with psychological matters, but in my personal life experiences. I wanted to continue to share my story and my knowledge with others in hopes that I can help someone-even if it's only one person-the journey that brought me to this point was worth it.

I continue to stress, this book is not a cure all. I don't proclaim to have the "inside scoop" on life. I don't consider myself to be above anyone in any way. I firmly believe that if *I* can do it, *anybody* can.

My life is far from perfect. I have struggles and trials just like everyone else. I have learned to handle things in a less destructive manner because I have been able to change my perception of how I view struggles and trials.

Again, I thank you from the bottom of my heart. My prayer is that you will go on to accomplish what others viewed impossible. My prayer is that one day someone will say, "Because of you, I didn't give up."

Love and Prayers,

Trina "TiTi Ladette" Cleveland

Resources/Helpful Info

In order to fulfill my desire to publish my first book, *The Pink Elephant in the Middle of the Getto*, I knew my story alone was not enough to provoke the change I'd like to see take place in our communities. As a corollary achievement to the book, I have went on to create a nonprofit organization that advocates for women and families who are undergoing the Child Protective Services (CPS) process, an institutional version of the book, and now this workbook.

I knew I had to research the subjects of molestation, addiction, and mental illness as it relates to African Americans; not that African Americans are the only ones who suffer in these areas, but because I happen to be African American and was born into a culture whose national anthem is, **"What goes on in this house stays in this house."**

I feel, based on my own experience, this golden rule is sure to get someone killed or cause more of our children to be abused, molested, and become damaged adults who abuse and neglect their children as well and further perpetuate the cycle.

As it relates to Molestation:

[1]*Although children of every gender, age, race, ethnicity, background, socio economic status and family structure are at risk, race and ethnicity are an important factor in identified sexual abuse. African American children have almost twice the risk of sexual abuse than white children.*

According to studies, there are more African American related cases of sexual abuse than any other ethnic group. I found this to be paradoxical since those same studies show that those cases often go unreported. Although it baffles me as to how they came up with this estimation, many researchers believe that it is because African Americans are used to bearing pain in a predominantly discriminatory society. They believe African Americans often view acts of molestation and abuse as somewhat a general course of life.

Child molesters of any ethnic group mainly molest children close to them. 85-95% of reported cases of sexual abuse involve a perpetrator known to the child, 35% involve a family member, and 50% of all sexual assaults take place in the home of the child or offender. The average offender is involved with over 70 children in his or her offending career.

Although sexual offenders have various circumstances that cause them to perpetrate, research shows that sexual abuse is mainly a "learned behavior" meaning they themselves were at one time victims of sexual abuse.

---

[1] Sexual Abuse (Darkness to Light.org),

As it relates to Physical Abuse:

Recent studies have shown that 89% of African Americans spank their children. Although people from other ethnic groups have been known to spank their children as well, most of those people have often spanked with an open hand, whereas African Americans often use an object, sometimes dangerous ones.

Some researchers believe that harsh whippings are a legacy "left by the brutality of slavery". Other researchers believe that African Americans have a more rigorous religious belief that reinforces the old saying "Spare the rod, spoil the child".

At any rate, a lot of times, spankings in our culture often border or cross the line to child abuse.

Statistics show that 95% of child abusers were abused themselves as children. The cycle seems to repeat itself when those victims of abuse have children as well.

Based on my personal experience, it is no longer acceptable for me to spank my children. Spankings and beatings were deeply entrenched in my psyche as the ultimate form of discipline that would bring about a desired result but because of my mental health issues, I couldn't differentiate the fine line of spankings and abuse.

I have also come to believe that it is impossible for me to teach my children that hitting someone or being hit by someone is unacceptable if I, myself, am hitting them.

As it relates to Addiction:

[2]*High risk factors for substance abuse disorders for African Americans, particularly the youth population include low self-esteem, low levels of family pride, and deviant peer associations. A family history of alcoholism has also been found to be a significant predictor of substance abuse for this population.*

Some minorities experience pervasive stress unique to their minority status that may contribute to their drug use, such as pressure to reconcile values of their culture of origin with those of mainstream American culture. Racism, discrimination, language barriers, and dealing with social service agencies have been associated with substance abuse disorders within minority populations.

For African American adolescent males in particular, drug dealing appears to be a significant risk factor for developing a substance use disorder.

---

[2] OSAS Retreatment of African Americans

Research demonstrates strong evidence between drug use, drug dealing, and homicide for the African American population.

This summation mirrored my own opinions in this regard to substance abuse. During my time living the street life, I was surrounded by young drug dealers, who themselves were addicts unbeknownst to them. They would smoke weed (which is now a days chemically enhanced), pop pills, and smoke wet (embalming fluid). The money they make dealing crack cocaine mainly goes to supply their own drug of choice. Jails and institutions are flooded with such type of young, Black males. They are also often gang related and get into turf wars with other gangs, which add to the homicide rate. Nearly half of all prisoners in the United States are African Americans. This is a vicious cycle that I hope one day will end.

As it relates to Mental Illness

[3]*The most common mental disorders involve depression, with nearly 20 million Americans suffering some form of major or mild depressive disorder. According to the **National Institute of Mental Health,** "Most likely, depression is caused by a combination of genetic, biological, environmental, and psychological factors. "Additionally, "Some genetics research indicates that risk for depression results from several genes acting together with environmental or other factors. In addition, trauma, loss of a loved one, a difficult relationship, or any stressful situation may trigger a depressive episode."*

*With Black Americans leading the country with troubling statistics in areas like **unemployment**, **child abuse and neglect**, and **domestic violence**, all of which can exacerbate stress, it is perhaps not surprising that the community leads the country in mental health struggles. According to the Center or Disease Prevention's **Office of Minority Health and Health Disparities**, African Americans are "still more likely to experience a mental disorder than their white counterparts "but less likely to seek treatment" though **Psychology Today** recently noted that there has been an increase in the number of Black Americans seeking treatment for ailments such as depression over the last decade. Men are less likely to seek treatment than women, regardless of race, meaning Black men are the least likely to seek treatment over all.*

Upon researching mental illness as it relates to African Americans, I was amazed at some of the facts I learned. With all the advancement in mental health care, it still plagues me why many more Black Americans do not seek out mental health care.

Another alarming mental health issue amongst Black Americans is bipolar disorder. Bipolar disorder, also known as Manic Depression, is an illness marked by severe mood swings-phases

---

3

http://www.theroot.com/articles/culture/2013/05/mental_health_illness_in_blacks_failure_to_seek_treatment_may_be_holding_us_back.html of euphoria and often depression. It is sometimes accompanied by schizoaffective disorder, a condition that includes chronic symptoms of schizophrenia and also episodes of affective disorder (either bipolar or depressive). This illness often goes undiagnosed and undetected in many Americans.

[4]While the rate of bipolar disorder is the same among African Americans as it is among other Americans, African Americans are less likely to receive a diagnosis and treatment for this illness because:

- A mistrust of health professionals.
- Cultural barriers between doctors and patients.
- Reliance on religious community during times of emotional distress.
- **A tendency to mask symptoms with substance abuse.**
- No health insurance. (25% of African Americans don't have health insurance).
- Continued misunderstanding and stigma about mental illness.

From my own experience, while I was academically gifted and creative in many ways, I have always struggled socially and emotionally as a result of my diagnosis of bipolar with schizoaffective disorder. And true to the fact stated above, I often masked my symptoms with drug use. I feel that the substance abuse further accelerated my chemical imbalance.

Other facts I discovered:

- [5]African Americans are disproportionately more likely to experience social circumstances that increase their chances of developing a mental illness.
- Children in foster care and the child welfare system are more likely to develop mental illnesses. (African American children comprise 45% of the public foster care population.)
- Nearly half of all prisoners in the United States are African American. Prison inmates are at a higher risk of developing a mental illness.
- Exposure to violence increases the risk of developing a mental illness. (Over 25% of African American children exposed to violence meet criteria for posttraumatic stress disorder.)

These facts were eye-opening for me. I realized how important my mental health was in regards to making healthy decisions for me and my children. It is important for us as Black Americans to seek mental health care. I believe this would alleviate some of the disparity we have in association to our children in foster care, our children abusing substances, and also passing down our misguided beliefs to our children, furthering the cycle of misinformation.

---

[4] NMHA.org
[5] National Alliance on Mental Illness (NAMI.org)

Many African American women who have suffered sexual abuse general have more suicidal thoughts and/or attempts, greater histories of inpatient mental health institutions, more years of cocaine use, and more problems due to substance abuse.

Many coping behaviors they use are: problem avoidance, wishful thinking, social withdrawal, and self-criticism. African American women with sexual abuse histories also have a more complex clinical picture. They have more severe psychiatric symptoms, more complex family histories, and more experience of a range of traumas.

We must begin the process of getting better by reevaluating our belief systems. Culturally, our belief systems have been passed down from generation to generation, and while we at some point upgrade these symptoms, our core beliefs traditionally center on those that were handed down.

Warning Signs of Sexual Abuse

- *Sudden change in mood or behavior.*
- *Trouble walking or sitting.*
- *Displays knowledge or interest in sexual acts inappropriate to his or her age, or even seductive behavior.*
- *Makes strong efforts to avoid a specific person without reason.*
- *An STD or pregnancy, especially under the age of fourteen.*
- *Runs away from home.*

Behavioral Signs of Sexual Abuse

- *Uncomfortable around or rejection of typical family affection.*
- *Problems in school.*
- *Reports of sexual assault.*

If you, or someone you know is the victim of child-hood sexual abuse you may contact:

National Child Sexual Abuse Hotline

Darkness to Light

1-866-FOR-LIGHT (866-367-5444)

        Or

Stop It Now

1-888-PREVENT (888-773-2362)

Or

The Childhood National Child Abuse Hotline

1-800-4-A-CHILD (800-422-4453)

For help with alcohol or chemical dependency call:

Alcohol and Drug Helpline (800-821-4357)

Alcohol and Drug Abuse Hotline (800-729-6686)

National Council on Alcoholism & Drug Dependence Hopeline (800-622-2255)

For a Mental Health Crisis

National Mental Health Association 800-969-NHMA (800-969-6642)

Trina "TiTi Ladette" Cleveland has found a new way to live through writing and poetry. Her gift was hidden for years as she struggled with addiction and mental illness.

TiTi is not only an author, she's an Inspirational/Motivational Speaker, a Spoken Word Artist, a Publisher, an Entrepreneur, and the President and Founder of her nonprofit: www.remembertothinkpink.org. She is also a full-time college student working towards a degree in Forensic Social Work.

Although she maintains she is new at Spoken Word, her poetry is real and relevant. She is living proof that no matter what life throws at you- you can get back up…again and again.

TiTi is a native of Austin, Texas and the mother of five children. After reclaiming her life, and publishing her first book, she received many requests for "the next one."

"A Pimp and a Prostitute…A Ghetto Love Story" was her debut into Urban Fiction and the first book in her Ghetto Love Story series. Although she is a socially conscious individual who lives her life based on spiritual principles, she felt that writing a collection of Urban Fiction would provide a creative outlet that would enable her to release the stories that live on the inside of her. Her Urban Fiction books will be written under her given name, "Trina Cleveland" as to not create a conflict in her ultimate message, "There is a better way to live."

As a nonprofit, her goals are to prevent child neglect and abuse by working directly with parents. She hopes to advocate for women who are going through the CPS process. Her nonprofit is the corollary achievement of her book which reminds parents that… "Before making a decision that will alter the life of your child, remember to….. ThinkPink!"

TiTi has now published four books including *The Pink Elephant in the Middle of the Getto, The Pink Elephant in the Middle of the Getto Workbook, The Pink Elephant in the Middle of the Getto Institutional Version, and her latest Urban Fiction book, "A Pimp and a Prostitute… A Ghetto Love Story"*

Her proceeds from her books will go to further the mission of her nonprofit: Remember To ThinkPink.

Please stay tuned for the upcoming stage play*: "The Pink Elephant in the Ghetto"*